SAVING THE CORPORATE DOLLAR

by

R.E. Manchester

authorHOUSE™

1663 LIBERTY DRIVE, SUITE 200
BLOOMINGTON, INDIANA 47403
(800) 839-8640
WWW.AUTHORHOUSE.COM

First published by AuthorHouse 10/05/05

ISBN: 1-4208-5711-8 (sc)

Library of Congress Control Number: 2005904321

Printed in the United States of America
Bloomington, Indiana

This book is printed on acid-free paper.

DISCLAIMER

This book is designed as a guide to provide accurate and thought provoking information on the subject of corporate business policies and finance. It is sold with the understanding that neither the Author nor the Publisher is engaged in the business of rendering accounting, legal or any other professional services by publishing this book. Questions relevant to corporate finance should be addressed to an appropriate professional. The Author and Publisher disclaim any liability, loss, or risk associated with the use and application of any of the contents of this book.

Acknowledgments

Many people inspired this book. Thank you to my family and friends that offered me encouragement while writing this book. To the many co-workers that not only demonstrated the utmost ambition and honest work ethics, but also to the people who showed me the underside of the work force. These people taught me the most about human nature and inspired this book.

Thank you to Lynette Wood for providing unlimited support and encouragement. To Tommy, Mike and Laurie Roberts for providing the inspiration to produce a high quality product. The future of our business culture and economy is with the young entrepreneurs of tomorrow. Thank you to Charles Coviello for teaching me the meaning of social responsibility at a young age. Thank you Val Bogner for the help with my writing calisthenics.

Thank you to Mary Pirozzoli, Jeanne & Russell Horvath for inspiration. To Adrienne Ruggiero, thank you for always remaining honest and professional. To Gloria Northop for friendship and advice. And a special thank you to my three friends who have provided companionship and happiness over the past few years.

Introduction

This book was started a few years ago. After being an entrepreneur, business owner and self-employed for many years, I was fed up with business. I had creative burn out and had been pretty beaten up by some unscrupulous business associates that had decimated my cash flow.

So I decided to pack it all in. I decided to start over at the bottom of the corporate ladder and get a job working for a local large corporation. I did not want any major responsibilities. I wanted a simple 9 to 5 job with no headaches.

To my surprise and chagrin at being a bit over qualified, they hired me. To even more of my surprise, I watched as millions of dollars of the corporation's money was squandered. As a former business owner and CEO, it appalled me. Waste was everywhere and no one seemed to care or pay attention to the problems.

Thinking it was a particular company and mismanagement, I changed jobs. But to my dismay, money problems were still evident in the new job that I started.

I started talking to other employees. They told me stories of different jobs where the waste and spending problems were even worse. Being in the ranks of the employees, but thinking as a business owner, I was able to gain a new perspective on why and how money was being lost.

Armed with the information of my few years of "working" research, I endeavored to write this book to help businesses save money. I have come to the conclusion that employees and management can't be blamed separately for wasting money. But they share the blame. As a team, the common goal should be to strive towards the prosperity of the business.

And what happened to the corporations that I worked for? They are no longer in business or a glimmer of their former majestic selves. And the government job I had? That's another story for another day.

TABLE OF CONTENTS

SAVING THE CORPORATE DOLLAR

In times of prosperity business owners don't usually take a hard look at expenses. They may know their bottom line, but most don't analyze it. Unfortunately, it takes hard times and lack of profits to make a company owner look at where all the money is going.

One of the major problems with corporate growth is that expenditures can get out of hand. In many cases owners of the company can have too strict controls over spending, which will impede growth. For example, an employee that does not have the authority to authorize an emergency purchase for your biggest client. The purchase isn't made, the product doesn't come in on time, and you lose the customer.

In other instances where controls are not put in place unlimited spending can take place. In most corporations five cents of every dollar goes to money that employees steal in some way or form. You may feel you have the most honest people in the world working for you, and even close relatives. But most employees take liberties with their jobs. Controls must be in place to make sure this doesn't happen.

Unscrupulous employees can order very expensive equipment and have it dropped shipped to their homes.

Uncontrolled spending most often is in the form of employees not doing their jobs. I have heard of employees that had lawn chairs set up on the roof of a building. They would duck out a side door, go up and sun bathe and read books for hours. The managers never missed them. Some employees would sleep for a few hours at their desk after lunch every day. One employee ran his real estate business from work and would disappear for hours while he went out to show houses. Many employees know about staircases or exits where they can slip in and out of work without anyone seeing them.

How can you avoid out of control spending? How can you avoid out of control employees? Knowledge. You need to know what is going on in the ranks of your business. You need information to trickle up to you through the people you hire. You need to know what is broken before you can fix it. *First task is you need to get every bit of data on every dime spent by your business.*

How Do I Fix It?

It is the worse case scenario. You are on the verge of bankruptcy. Your employees are looting the company. What do you do? First thing to do is you need to find out where your money is going. Look at your profit and loss statements. Before you can fix the money "leaks" you will need to know where and what you are spending the money on. What are your major expenditures? How can you cut them? There are <u>always</u> ways to cut down on expenditures. You may not like having to do so. It may be uncomfortable seeing that you have made erroneous decisions in a previous year's budget. To be able to fix the problems you need to realize that you can always cut back spending money on something. Follow these three basic rules:

1) Find out where the money is going.
2) Find out why the money is being spent in that manner.
3) Assess the needs of the company and cut back on spending.

Notice that you need to assess the needs of the company. What are your minimum operating costs? How can you cut that in half? Sometimes the need of the company to exist will depend solely on your ability to cut your costs.

The next part is pretty easy. Identify where the money is going.

One of the problems with cutting overhead costs is that many costs fall into this category. To understand exactly where these costs are coming from and who is spending the money, you need to break the costs out into separate categories.

To analyze these costs you should have a spreadsheet in front of you with every cent broken into categories such as cell phones, expense accounts, courier services, limousine services, air travel, utilities, newspaper subscriptions and about a hundred more categories as needed.

Slashing expenses is a bit more difficult. Determine how much you want to save and disallow any expenses that you deem inappropriate. Vanquish expense accounts. Eliminate company credit cards. Make strict requirements on costs that are to be reimbursed.

You can start cutting costs, once you know what they are and who is spending the money.

Hire a Professional

Saving the corporate dollar should start as a standard practice when the business opens. Nothing is more important as knowing where your money is, and where it is being spent. A trained purchasing professional can usually handle company purchases and use competitive bids and price analysis. If you don't have a professional purchasing agent or buyer, hire one. They can save you the cost of their salary many times over in a year's time. Price, speed of delivery and quality are the three elements of a purchase that most purchasing professionals will weigh and act on. If you can't justify the expense of an additional salary, find a company that will buy for you. Some businesses now specialize in group purchases.

Do not leave purchases up to administrative assistants. Most people buy for convenience when using other people's money. Buying for convenience is the fastest way to fill the order and get the job done. Price is usually a non-priority.

Hiring an auditor or cost analyst at $50-$150 per hour may also be a good way to find out where money on expenditures is falling through the cracks of your organization. Perhaps you only need to hire a temporary purchasing professional to set up software that will automate the purchases for your office.

How Do I Know If I Should Buy From a Specific Vendor?

If you have purchased goods from a vendor in the past, you may need a way to evaluate their performance. *This evaluation chart will help to identify if you should continue to buy from a vendor that has had problems with delivery, quality or cost.*

By purchasing from vendors that fall into the light (M) median shaded areas, and eliminating the vendors that fall into the dark shaded areas, you will have less chance of future problems. This chart is a very good indicator of the future performance of vendors when you have a critical project. It also may be used to compare vendors of the same product.

Assign a number that represents your vendor's Past Performance/History from the column numbers. Then find a number that represents delivery/quality/cost from the row lists below. Follow those numbers to an intersecting block on the chart to find if your vendor has fallen into a median (M) area of acceptable history and quality of performance.

Column Numbers
Represent Vendor Past Performance and History
(Assign a number from the left column in the chart below)
1-Significant Problems in the past
2-Some problems have occurred
3-Anticipates problems
4-Have avoided problems
5-Will avoid problems

Matrix for Purchases

	1	2	3	4	5	
5	M	M				
4		M	M			
3		M	M			
2						
1						
	1	2	3	4	5	

Row Numbers
Represent Vendor Delivery/Quality/Cost
(Assign a number across the bottom row)
1-Not an issue
2-Acceptable
3-Acceptable with minor problems
4-Major problems, costs, and delays
5-Unacceptable

BEWARE OF HIDDEN COSTS

If you are buying an item, you know what you are buying. Correct? Not always. If you are buying an item, you should see the invoice or bill to make sure that you are only being billed for that specific item. It is very important to match invoices with orders. Vendors have a funny way of trying to increase their profits at your expense. This can involve adding mysterious charges to your order such as; excess shipping fees, minimum order fee, delivery charge, handling charges, surcharge, service fees, reclamation or recycling charges, and incorrect quantities or prices. Always look at your invoice and verify that it is exactly what you have agreed to pay.

Work with Vendors

Many people perceive a vendor as an obstacle that needs to be conquered. A vendor should be a working partner, not someone who is looked upon as a problem to overcome.

Open channels of communication with all of your vendors. Have meetings with the sales people or district managers. Tell them that you need to cut costs and ask them to suggest ways to do so. Many times a vendor has knowledge about new products or a means to incorporate savings.

Co-Op Buying

Companies miss the opportunity to take advantage of co-op buying. Co-op buying is when a few companies join forces to make bulk purchases that will lower their prices on a product. Most vendors will offer a "Price Break" or a lower price on an item once you buy the item in a larger quantity. Some may also offer a lower cost if you request bulk packaging.

Talk to your friends and fellow business people to find out if they would like to form a buying club. If a few companies join, you may be able to realize hundreds to thousands of dollars in savings per year. Joining a local Chamber of Commerce will help you to find local vendors and help save money.

Renting
Computer Equipment
Instead of Buying

Computer obsolescence and depreciation happens so fast that in some cases it would be more cost effective to rent a "State of the art" computer for a year instead of buying one. Perhaps you only need to rent a computer for a special project that would last a few months. Renting can be more flexible than leasing.

An electronic letterhead or company forms may be more cost effective than printing or copying. Keep an inventory of electronic read-only forms on your computer for distribution as needed.

COMPUTER CENTER & WEB SITE DESIGN

Most companies have a web site integrated into their IT operations. Why? Because it easily falls into the category of Information Technology.

Wrong move.

A web page is a creative, advertising instrument that is used for many purposes. It shouldn't be the responsibility of computer professionals.

In most cases a web page can be used to market your company, bring in customers and share information. The responsibility of designing and content should come from the creative heads of your company.

After you decide the objectives you would like to achieve with your web site, bring in your computer engineers. Tell them what you would like to do. Then stand back and watch them tell you that they can't do it with their current resources!

Computer professionals like to have state of the art equipment. The major problem with this, is the fact that all computer equipment is obsolete a week after you purchase it. You need to understand that your computer pro-fessionals will <u>NEVER</u> be satisfied with the equipment they have. Computer equipment should be purchased with growth in mind.

Once you have a blue print for your web page design, try out-sourcing the design work. Try asking around a college or computer techni-cal school. Students will design your web page for a fraction of the cost and for the experi-ence. Most would jump at the opportunity to be able to include it on their resume. You may also work out an intern deal.

After your page is designed, you will need to decide where it will be hosted. If you happen to have a server hanging around, not being used, no problem. But don't go out and buy computer equipment to host your web page. Have it hosted through a hosting company.

Outsource

As we discussed previously, it pays to outsource your web hosting and possibly your entire computer services department or help desk. It is now possible to outsource almost every department in your corporation. There are companies that will do your HR, Payroll, maintenance and facilities management. You can even find outside sales representatives that work on a commission basis to sell your product.

Brain storming and thinking "Outside the box" helps in deciding if you would like to outsource various resources. Knowing your numbers and department costs will give you the information needed to make this decision.

Consider the following scenario:
You wake up one morning and the entire payroll department who had all chipped in on a ticket, won the state lottery for $100 million dollars. They all just called in and quit their jobs. You have no payroll employees.

After kicking yourself for not chipping in a dollar to the payroll lottery pool, what do you do? You can't hire and train an entire department in a week. So you get out the Yellow Pages and start calling payroll services. *Because payroll services can get the work done on time and correctly.*

Most companies won't run into this type of winning lottery situation. But this example shows how you can efficiently outsource services. You have no employee costs, no related overhead costs, no training costs, and no employee turn over.

The key to saving money by outsourcing is knowing what each employee costs and the overall costs involving the department. Factor in the convenience of having it in house, along with the performance of the employees and the costs of computer equipment, phones, copiers, and support equipment.

Buying Surplus Stock and Auctions

Many companies buy used goods. This is a huge cost savings when it comes to office supplies, office furniture, and inventory. Talk to your suppliers and try to find out where your competition buys their inventory. Talk to your competition and see if they are willing to trade surplus inventory or machinery. The opportunity can arise almost from anywhere to save money.

Look in newspapers for bankruptcy notices; Government auctions and business close outs, even storage sales. These can be sources of huge bargains. At auctions you can pay pennies on the dollar for commodities that are valuable to your business either as consumerable goods or inventory. If you have excess items when you buy in bulk, you can sell the items on an online auction and generate income from them. One important fact to remember is that the name of the game is to save money. Buying in bulk is justified if the expenditure will save a good amount of money. You must know what you will be saving.

Example

Pallets of new trash bags are up for auction at an office supply auction. The pallet contains 50 boxes of industrial trash bags containing 100 bags per box. You can buy the pallet for $200.00.

You currently use 5 bags a week in your office and they cost .50 per bag.

If you buy these trash bags at the auction, it will bring your cost per bag down to .04 each. Your savings per year will be $119.60. And you will have enough bags for 19 years!

A Few Things to Remember

Before you bid, you must always know how much you are paying for an item so that you will be able to recognize opportunities and bargains. Make sure you do research before you go to an auction. Know what you need, how much you normally pay, and do not buy any items on impulse. In this particular case, you may want to sell half the bags (perhaps at .25 per bag). And you need to know in advance if you have adequate storage facilities for them.

Have Extra Inventory?

Try selling it on an Internet auction. Many companies have given up having online discount stores in favor of selling on an online auction service. One person assigned to listing auctions may be able to move mountains of inventory that have been gathering dust.

Think outside the box. Don't always try to solve money problems by standard corporate procedures. Test new suggestions for saving money. Reward and praise employees that suggest ways to save money.

EXPENSE ACCOUNTS RUN AMUCK?

Expense accounts can get out of hand if not handled correctly. One way to reduce expenses charged is to require all expenses to be prepaid by the employee on a *personal* credit card, not a company card. The expenses are turned in and approved by a reviewer. If an item is not approved, it is not reimbursed. Most employees will think twice about charging an item if they feel it may not be reimbursed. This will also put the financial burden on the employee should they not turn in supportive paperwork on time.

Always remember to implement ethics training and have it given to all employees on a yearly basis. Make sure you take the training first to understand what your employees are being taught.

Executive Waste

Are your expense accounts through the roof? Employee perks costing more and more each year? Many corporations are now stuck once they have given employees the red carpet treatment to lure them into your corporation. The only problem is now it can threaten to bankrupt your corporation.

Executives waste more time and money than their lower paid counterparts. They are given expense accounts, cars, more vacations, higher pay and less supervision. In most cases their managers are as unconcerned with things such as the bottom line, as they are.

A simple executive rule, the more money they make, the more money they can waste.

If you are cutting corners in your corporation, look to the executives first. Lose the company cars, the expense accounts, and credit cards. Make them account for their time. Don't let them get complacent. For every lazy, wasteful executive you have on your payroll that spends his day reading the sports page of the newspaper, or planning out his fantasy baseball team, there are four college students willing to take a quarter of his pay and none of the perks.

Before you decide to fire all your executives and hire a bunch of college students, let's look at some of the positive aspects of your executive staff. Some may seem very dedicated and willing to try new ideas. There is not a substitute for experience, and top executives bring with them experience and in may cases, clients. One solution would be to match top executives with younger executives. Let them train the younger execs. But it is up to you not to let the younger executives pick up their bad habits.

A corporation needs to take a proactive stance with executives. Keep them on their toes, motivated and hungry. Make them punch a time clock and let them know someone is looking over their shoulder.

Finances

Recently I interviewed Mary who has worked for a very successful chain of stores for over 20 years. She is head of the payroll department and oversees the distribution of hundreds of checks each week. I asked her how her department has saved money for the company over the years.

She reported that the most important way that her department has saved money is by not making mistakes in the payroll. Mistakes cost money. Any time an error occurs, a new way to check for that error is instituted so it will not happen again. She stated that every check that is issued goes through many processes. It is checked numerous times for accuracy so that all funds and deductions are completely balanced and correct. Over the years her Payroll Department worked to reduce their mistakes down to 3 in 100,000 checks. All of this has been accomplished by running a strict series of tests to insure that everything is correct.

This demonstrates the fact that we need to know where our money is, and exactly how it is spent. Mistakes cost money. Install tight controls, check and balance systems, reduce errors and stop losing money.

Meeting Costs

How many meeting have you slept through? How many meetings have you been bored? Unfortunately, not all speakers are interesting and thought provoking. And not all subjects can hold your attention. Most meetings run too long. Try to keep meetings short so that people's attention span is engaged. Encourage discussion via email after the meeting ends.

Meetings have become a way for employees to waste time. The usual meeting consists of a few people speaking and many people listening. Perhaps an email blast can be used to relay messages instead of having everyone attend a meeting.

If you need time to discuss important matters schedule it during lunch. Supply an inexpensive lunch such as pizza or sandwiches or have an informal meeting where employees bring their own lunch. You can also schedule a meeting an hour before the work day ends or right after the work day ends such as 5:30 PM. People are anxious to get home and will end the meeting on time and keep subjects short. This will cut down on wasted time.

Another way to keep a meeting short is to have everyone stand during the meeting. Have all the chairs removed from the room prior to the meeting. It changes the dynamics of the room incredibly. This will usually limit how long people will speak and keep you on a faster track.

One expense for companies that in the past could not be cut was the cost of meetings. A company was saddled with the cost of flying employees into a central meeting place and paying for accommodations. With web conferencing these cost are no longer a huge expense. Meetings can be held with rented telecomm, web conferencing equipment or just a computer. Even training can be held through virtual classrooms online.

Try out Placewhere.com or GotoMeeting. com. These web sites will allow you to have a company wide meeting online without any wasted travel expenses.

You may want to experiment with having meetings online after normal work hours. This will provide you with important data. It will show you the people who are dedicated to their job and ambitious. Most of the time, people who are lazy or not motivated will miss these meetings. The sacrifice of personal time is a good barometer of commitment to the company. But do not take advantage of it.

Advisors

"A prince, therefore, ought always to take counsel, but only when he wishes and not when others wish; he ought rather to discourage every one from offering advice unless he asks it; but, however, he ought to be a constant inquirer, and afterwards a patient listener concerning the things of which he inquired; also, on learning that nay one, on any consideration, has not told him the truth, he should let his anger be felt."
Niccolo Machiavelli *The Prince*

Surround yourself with a group of experts in every field. Never stop looking for new people to add to this list. This list will become an important tool. Sit down at your computer and make a list or database that lists all types of professionals that cover all phases of business and their contact information. These people can be relatives, friends or casual acquaintances. They should be people that you are comfortable to talk with. They should include; Lawyers, Tax Experts, Insurance Agents, Real Estate Agents, Business Owners, Computer Professionals, Teachers, Engineers. Any field can be helpful, so list everyone you know and their field of expertise. This group of people will be your free source of advice. Before you make major decisions, look to these people for guidance. Call them and ask questions, ask them as many questions as you can about their subject. Pick their brains. If a particular person does not have an answer to your question, ask them to refer you to someone that would know. Not many people have made poor decisions by having too much information. The more information you have on a subject, the more you can make an objective decision.

Remember to thank your experts. Take them out to lunch or send them flowers or ball game tickets. Offer your help or advice should they need it.

Never ask someone a question if they could have a financial gain depending on how they answer the question. Money very often will cloud one's objectivity.

THE IMPORTANCE OF HAVING A TRUE SOUNDING BOARD

Poor decisions will cost company money. The decision to add new lines, grow into new markets, and even to move to a new location can cost money and possibly mean failure for a business.

The importance of having a few close friends and acquaintances that will be painfully truthful with you can't be stressed enough. As a company executive or CEO there are not many people who do not depend on you for their income. They do not want to offend you; it could cost them their job. If you happen to come up with an "Off the wall" idea people may not respond truthfully.

I have been lucky to have a close friend named Gloria. I will bounce an idea off of her and she will argue the feasibility of the idea into infinity. Needless to say, I get frustrated, angry, mad, yell and scream while turning beet red. This is all in defense of my idea while she pokes holes into it. While not great for my blood pressure, it is great for business.
Gloria doesn't hold an MBA, but she knows business and I highly respect her opinion. So, as she engages me in an all out attack on my

idea, I start to see all of the flaws and possible pitfalls. In some cases I can overcome the obstacles and go on as planned, but in other instances, by debating and defending the validity of the idea, I find in the long run, it is not such a grand idea.

By having someone you can discuss ideas with, that are not on your payroll, you can get an objective opinion. By having someone play devil's advocate, they can help you to see the down side of your idea or plans. This is very important in decision-making. Never underestimate the value of opposition.

Time Constraints

Many CEO's are made ineffective by the lack of prioritizing duties during the day. Many are reactive not proactive in running a company. One of the chief complaints is "I can never get anything done because my phone is constantly ringing"

To be able to manage a company effectively, you need to be able to manage your time. If the telephone interrupts your thought process or your work, you need to turn off your cell phone and office ringer. Let all calls go into voice mail and return calls at a later time. It is easy to get sucked into putting out fires all day long and micromanaging the small problems. A lot of the time small problems can be the result of a much larger problem that needs to be addressed.

Prioritize

Being able to manage your time means that you need to take control of your time and how it is spent. You need to be aware of the passing of time and your schedule. Successful people find that making lists will help you to prioritize the items you need to tend to during the day. Personal organizers, Day planners and even just pen and paper can help to list things you need to do. After you list all the items that should be done during the day, you need to prioritize them according to importance and how critical it is to complete the specific task. A time that you feel is sufficient to complete each task should be assigned to each item. Most people underestimate how long it will take to complete each task. Other people end up postponing tasks they don't want to do and rolling them over from one day to another.

To be able to complete the items on your list you need to be honest with yourself. Interruptions need to be stopped. You may even want to find a secluded area to work so you have no distractions. Understand that you may not be able to do everything on your list and be flexible enough to move tasks to another day. However, if you find that you have rolled a particular task to another day for a few weeks, you need to address that issue. Why are you not getting to finish that item? If it is an unpleasant task for you, try delegating it to another person. You may also want to ask someone to work on it with you on a specific date and time. If you commit to another person to work on something, sometimes it will help to get that task started.

Many people go through life like the little kid who did their Science Project the night before it was due, even though they had a month to complete it. Procrastination can stagnate and impede forward motion in a company. Growth needs nurturing and care to details. Not doing your job or glossing over issues can result in small problems growing into bigger problems. Putting good work habits into place not only sets a good example for the rest of your work force, it also will help you to set and see your goal clearly. It is sometimes easy to see where you want to be, but you can't always see the path. By planning ahead in steps, it will get you into the habit of thinking through each of the steps needed to achieve your goals.

The Buck Stops Here.

If the owner or CEO of a company sets a positive example for cost savings, most employees will follow the example. As owner of a company, do not flaunt non-essential expenditures. Sure, a corporate jet is nice. Some owners perceive it as showing the prosperity of the company to potential clients. But be careful of the image you are portraying. Most employees perceive extravagance as wasted money that could be used to increase their salary or improve working conditions.

Many CEOs take cuts in salary when a company starts to falter. I equate this to locking the barn after the cow has escaped. A CEO should be well aware of the financial status of their company. They should have their fingertip on the financial pulse of the company at all times. If it is a 3 or 300,000 employee business, the finances are the lifeblood of the business. It is a simple fact, that if you are not making money, you will go out of business. Larger businesses are able to delay this inevitable event by borrowing or shifting money, but it will happen. The only way to be able to make it in any business is to make more money than you spend. One of the major keys in business is to know your financial health in advance and plan accordingly. Know business cycles or when to expect a lull in sales.

You need to be as adept at planning for down sizing as you are for growth because either may happen at any time. And with economical cycles running a roller coaster ride as they have in the past three decades you can count on both these events happening to you.

EMPLOYEES

An often-overlooked item in a corporation is the employee's wages. This is overlooked because most employers think that wages are fixed, salaries are fixed, and nothing can ever change.

This would be the case if each employee were given an employment offer letter spelling out his or her wages, vacation, and perks. But times bring along change and if an employee is employed at will; their conditions of employment can change if it is implemented with all employees, meaning a company wide change.

Raises should always be merit based and not tenure based. People need to earn wages and be praised and rewarded for good work.

What is the No. 1 thing a business can do to make employees feel more valued? You get better work out of people if you praise them on a regular basis when they have earned it. That means each individual needs some words of praise, not a team or group of people. This kind of praise needs to be specific, and consistent. It must also be genuine.

One of the most useful measures of an employee's productiveness, which is becoming completely obsolete, is the time clock.

There is absolutely no reason why a corporation should not monitor when a person is "On the clock". One of the biggest ways a person can take advantage of a company is by robbing them of "time".

Extended lunches, coming in late and leaving early can all be monitored. It makes the employee more conscious of the company's time. Even if you do not monitor the time cards, the employees will think you do, thus improving productivity. Have time cards apply towards all employees, even executives. Executives usually abuse time the most.

Vacation days can be added or subtracted during the year, but watch out for morale problems if vacation days are cut. Sometimes a weekly seasonal shut down is better than cutting vacation days. The employees can collect a week or two of unemployment benefits and enjoy the time off. The company can then appreciate the lowered operating expenses for a few weeks.

Overpaid individuals should be scrutinized to determine if they are worth what they are being paid.

Do they pay for themselves in the work output?

Can you pay someone else less money to do the same job?

These questions must be answered to analyze their worth.

Sometimes taking one person's job responsibilities and splitting them up between two people will help you to reduce manpower needed to run your business.

Can the person who answers the phone also coordinate the deliveries?

Use your imagination to combine jobs and possibly departments.

Watch employees to see who has valuable work habits. These employees come in on time, only take an hour lunch and produce tangible work each day. These are your top performers and assets. Hold on to them, they set a valuable example for other employees.

SHAKE UP THE DEPARTMENTS

Complacency is a recipe for disaster. Employees that have been doing the same job for years will find efficient ways to shorten the time it takes to do the job, allowing them more time to relax or socialize. It is the employer's responsibility to make sure each person is utilizing time to the fullest. Not stretching out tasks to fill up time. Delegate more responsibility to the employees. Offer incentives such as afternoons off, if deadlines are met days ahead of time. In the long run, you may end up saving money by offering time off if a critical task is completed.

Frederick Winslow Taylor wrote of employee "Soldiering" or loafing in a paper he wrote in 1903. The same element of human nature exists in our current corporate office environments.

"The writer therefore quotes herewith from a paper read before The American Society of Mechanical Engineers, in June, 1903, entitled "Shop Management," which it is hoped will explain fully this cause for soldiering:

"This loafing or soldiering proceeds from two causes. First, from the natural instinct and tendency of men to take it easy, which may be called natural soldiering. Second, from more intricate second thought and reasoning caused by their relations with other men, which may be called systematic soldiering.

"There is no question that the tendency of the average man (in all walks of life) is toward working at a slow, easy gait, and that it is only after a good deal of thought and observation on his part or as a result of example, conscience, or external pressure that he takes a more rapid pace.

"There are, of course, men of unusual energy, vitality, and ambition who naturally choose the fastest gait, who set up their own standards, and who work hard, even though it may be against their best interests. But these few uncommon men only serve by forming a contrast to emphasize the tendency of the average.

"This common tendency to 'take it easy' is greatly increased by bringing a number of men together on similar work and at a uniform standard rate of pay by the day.

"Under this plan the better men gradually but surely slow down their gait to that of the poorest and least efficient. When a naturally *energetic man works for a few days beside a lazy one, the logic of the situation is unanswerable. 'Why should I work hard when that lazy fellow gets the same pay that I do and does only half as much work?'*

"A careful time study of men working under these conditions will disclose facts which are ludicrous as well as pitiable.

"To illustrate: The writer has timed a naturally energetic workman who, while going and coming from work, would walk at a speed of from three to four miles per hour, and not infrequently trot home after a day's work. On arriving at his work he would immediately slow down to a speed of about one mile an hour. When, for example, wheeling a loaded wheelbarrow, he would go at a good fast pace even up hill in order to be as short a time as possible under load, and immediately on the return walk slow down to a mile an hour, improving every opportunity for delay short of actually sitting down. In order to be sure not to do more than his lazy neighbor, he would actually tire himself in his effort to go slow.

"These men were working under a foreman of good reputation and highly thought of by his employer, who, when his attention was called to this state of things, answered: 'Well, I can keep them from sitting down, but the devil

can't make them get a move on while they are at work.'

"The natural laziness of men is serious, but by far the greatest evil from which both workmen and employers are suffering is the systematic soldiering which is almost universal under all of the ordinary schemes of management and which results from a careful study on the part of the workmen of what will promote their best interests.

"The writer was much interested recently in hearing one small but experienced golf caddy boy of twelve explaining to a green caddy, who had shown special energy and interest, the necessity of going slow and lagging behind his man when he came up to the ball, showing him that since they were paid by the hour, the faster they went the less money they got, and finally telling him that if he went too fast the other boys would give him a licking.

"This represents a type of systematic soldiering which is not, however, very serious, since it is done with the knowledge of the employer, who can quite easily break it up if he wishes.

"The greater part of the systematic soldiering, however, is done by the men with the deliberate object of keeping their employers ignorant of how fast work can be done.

"So universal is soldiering for this purpose that hardly a competent workman can be found in a large establishment, whether he works by the day or on piece work, contract work, or under any of the ordinary systems, who does not devote a considerable part of his time to studying just how slow he can work and still convince his employer that he is going at a good pace.

"The causes for this are, briefly, that practically all employers determine upon a maximum sum which they feel it is right for each of their classes of employees to earn per day, whether their men work by the day or piece.

"Each workman soon finds out about what this figure is for his particular case, and he also realizes that when his employer is convinced that a man is capable of doing more work than he has done, he will find sooner or later some way of compelling him to do it with little or no increase of pay.

"Employers derive their knowledge of how much of a given class of work can be done in a day from either their own experience, which has frequently grown hazy with age, from casual and unsystematic observation of their men, or at best from records which are kept, showing the quickest time in which each job has been done.

"In many cases the employer will feel almost certain that a given job can be done faster than it has been, but he rarely cares to take the drastic measures necessary to force men to do it in the quickest time, unless he has an actual record proving conclusively how fast the work can be done.

"It evidently becomes for each man's interest, then, to see that no job is done faster than it has been in the past. The younger and less experienced men are taught this by their elders, and all possible persuasion and social pressure is brought to bear upon the greedy and selfish men to keep them from making new records which result in temporarily increasing their wages, while all those who come after them are made to work harder for the same old pay.

"Under the best day work of the ordinary type, when accurate records are kept of the amount of work done by each man and of his efficiency, and when each man's wages are raised as he improves, and those who fail to rise to a certain standard are discharged and a fresh supply of carefully selected men are given work in their places, both the natural loafing and systematic soldiering can be largely broken up.

"This can only be done, however, when the men are thoroughly convinced that there is no

intention of establishing piece work even in the remote future, and it is next to impossible to make men believe this when the work is of such a nature that they believe piece work to be practicable. In most cases their fear of making a record which will be used as a basis for piece work will cause them to soldier as much as they dare.

"It is, however, under piece work that the art of systematic soldiering is thoroughly developed; after a workman has had the price per piece of the work he is doing lowered two or three times as a result of his having worked harder and increased his output, he is likely entirely to lose sight of his employer's side of the case and become imbued with a grim determination to have no more cuts if soldiering can prevent it. "Unfortunately for the character of the workman, soldiering involves a deliberate attempt to mislead and deceive his employer, and thus upright and straightforward workmen are compelled to become more or less hypocritical. The employer is soon looked upon as an antagonist, if not an enemy, and the mutual confidence which should exist between a leader and his men, the enthusiasm, the feeling that they are all working for the same end and will share in the results is entirely lacking.

"The feeling of antagonism under the ordinary piece-work system becomes in many cases so

marked on the part of the men that any proposition made by their employers, however reasonable, is looked upon with suspicion, and soldiering becomes such a fixed habit that men will frequently take pains to restrict the product of machines which they are running when even a large increase in output would involve no more work on their part."

As Frederick Winslow Taylor reported:

"Under the best day work of the ordinary type, when accurate records are kept of the amount of work done by each man and of his efficiency, and when each man's wages are raised as he improves, and those who fail to rise to a certain standard are discharged and a fresh supply of carefully selected men are given work in their places, both the natural loafing and systematic soldiering can be largely broken up."

As we apply this to today's work environment, we see some employees that are not efficient and producing sub standard work. These people need to be replaced, and higher standards of work expected from all employees. It is a way of "Raising the bar" and expecting the most from all of your employees.

Keeping Your Talent

Human Resource Management is taught at all the top business schools. What they don't teach you is proven methods on how to keep your top talent.

Ms. Lynette Wood, who teaches Human Resource Management to MBA students, refers to this talent as "Your Gold".

"Without your gifted employees, without your talented leaders, workers, idea people, motivators, silent but hard workers, you are lost. You may have the best product in the world but without the troops behind you, you can do nothing with it. Turnover costs in many ways, we know.

"How do you keep your talent? Recent research by the Gallup Poll and broadcast on NPR (National Public Radio) reported on an extensive survey the Gallup Poll conducted. They spoke directly to hundreds of managers and individuals seeking information on why they would stay and why they would leave a job. The top reason is not in the HR Management books. The major cause for someone staying or leaving their job is their immediate supervisor.

"Think about how much your immediate supervisor impacts your life, your work, and your day.

The following five items are what they also needed:

1. Do you know what is expected of you?
2. Do you have someone in the organization that mentors you?
3. Do you have the tools to do your work?
4. Do you feel you are cared about?
5. Do you feel challenged?"

Ms. Wood also added the following advice for employees to advance in the ranks of a company:
"Look for a mentor. The mentor does not have to be formal mentor program, simply have coffee with someone you respect and ask him or her a few questions. Someone who is honest and takes an interest in you qualifies as a mentor. If you can't identify someone, interview an executive in the company that you think highly of. Keep in touch with him/her once a month. Make a mentoring relationship happen. Ask a question; show your interest in the business. Executives like people that are motivated by more than just the paycheck. They are looking for people that are ambitious. They will make up the future management team.

"If you don't have the tools appropriate for doing your work, then speak up. List the tools, price them out and also put down how it will increase productively and use numbers. They say numbers talk, so here is a perfect place for them to talk and get you the tools.

Need motivation or more education? Look for an appropriate workshop and provide your superior with that information and why they should spend this money on you. How will it increase production or your work?

"Ask if you can work at home one day a month? Half a day, every other Friday? Is there a dress down day? Ask for it. Suggestion box? This helps communications, provides people with information from other departments and can be fun."

Management vs. Leadership

Managers manage problems, leaders lead people. In many work environments we have managers in positions that require a leader. We need to assess the requirements of a supervisory position to see if the services at hand are to simply manage people, or lead them. Leadership requires a person that has vision, perseverance and little bit of moxie thrown in to the mix. A manager is more of a problem solver who does not need to initiate forward motion. Always be careful not to put a manager into a leader's job. Do some self-assessment. Are you a manager or a leader? Can you lead your company towards the direction it needs to go? Do you need to hire someone to lead the company in this direction?

A true leader can visualize where the company will be in the future. The goals and dreams are tangible items in their mind. The steps to get to that point only need to be performed. So, it becomes a matter of fulfilling tasks to achieve a predetermined outcome.

Share the Vision

When a business is formed it is usually formed with a vision. The vision is the blueprint of where the business stands and where it is headed.

It is important to review your vision and to make sure it is still relevant. If the vision needs to be revised, then revise it! Share the vision with everyone in the company. Make sure they are aware of where you stand and where you want to go. It is very important to have every employee "on the same page," as well as making sure your vision is 100% correct.

Communication is the key to sharing the vision. If you want to have your entire organization behind you, they have to know what you are thinking. Miscommunication and loose interpretation of what you mean can lead to wasted time and money.
Put your vision statement on mugs, pens, and walls! Every single employee needs to know what the statement is and what you intend it to mean.

The vision is a very serious statement that mirrors your company's outlook on it's future.

It needs to be a true statement. Caution needs to be given in changing the vision statement. Since it is a serious business matter, it needs to be very well thought out before it is changed. And not changed arbitrarily. It should not be changed more than once every few years and it needs to invoke good moral and camaraderie along with customer service.

MOTIVATION

How motivated are your employees? Are they spending spare time looking for a new job on the Internet? Try to create an atmosphere of team spirit in the workplace. Have potluck lunches, have a bake sale and donate the proceeds to a local charity. Start a corporate bowling league or softball team. How about a babysitting club? If you expect an employee to dedicate time and creativity to your business, you need to reciprocate with more than a paycheck, and that need not cost a lot of money. Create a feeling of family and belonging. Team building will help to create this.

How are your work areas set up? Do you have your employees in cubicles? Think about reconfiguring your office set up. Would a web cam give each employee with a computer a magnificent view from your roof? Ask for suggestions from the employees. Vote on the suggestions. Studies have proven that even a change in lighting will improve productivity. Some people thrive in being with other people, while some people like to work alone. Try to accommodate these differences and you will see a huge difference in productivity.

BUILDING BLOCKS

In many cases having an in house seminar will fortify and strengthen teams within an organization. A motivational speaker can help address internal issues and completely turn an entire business into a mean fighting machine within hours. Do not use canned seminars; they will not address specific problems that you may have with your work force. An excellent company is Executive Solutions (203) 520-1075. They will give a free consultation and develop team building or a custom seminar encompassing issues that your employees may have. This expenditure is well worth the results.

"You're Fired"

This phrase may be your final solution to cutting expenses and motivation.

In the "Art of War" by Sun Tzu, disobedience in the ranks was handled by the "Middle Managers" being executed. This action was used as a warning. It demonstrated that no one is immune from discipline and managers must face the consequences if their teams do not perform.

When a situation reaches a point where there cannot be positive results from non-performing employees, you need to fire the employees that are not performing to your standards. Make sure you know why they are not performing. Poor management? Poor leadership? Loafing? Complacency? This move will be beneficial in sending a message to all employees that non-performance will not be tolerated. Motivation can be gleamed from this situation by letting the employees know that the organization is built on hard working, dedicated individuals.

Before you fire teams of employees, make sure you know the costs involved in replacing and/or retraining individuals to take over their positions. You may be able to redistribute the work among other employees at a cost savings.

Sinking Ships

In the mid 1800's when creaky old wooden cargo ships started to take on sea water and sink, one of the ways the sea farers would know that there was trouble aboard would be to watch the rats start to abandon the ship. They would crawl down the lines into the water, and try to swim to shore. It's true today in the corporate world. When a corporation starts to falter and sink, the biggest rats can still be seen jumping from the ship first.

When a company starts to make changes in their spending habits, such as limiting expense accounts or watching their money very closely, many times this is perceived by the employees as a danger sign. If in the past money was spent unwisely, the employees will wonder why constraints are now being made on spending. Employees may think the business is going bankrupt. It is important to reassure concerns about the welfare of the company. Explain why cuts are being made and why new policies are being introduced. It should be looked upon as a rebirth of a company and positive changes. You can also expect some employees who are not happy with budget cuts to leave. This winnowing of the employees is good for the company. You want to have employees that have respect for the company and its goals and policies.

Expand Your Horizons

Build more profit and bring in more business. Expand your market area. Golden opportunities may be found in different markets where consumers have not been properly serviced, where there may be confusion in market share, or the competition has become complacent. These opportunities are perfect examples of how to find a chink in your competition's armor.

Think out of the box when examining your competition. What are they doing correctly? What are they doing wrong? Strategic thinking on these two subjects can help you to increase business and avoid making mistakes.

Respond to change in positive and deliberate ways. Some people just hate change; they are reluctant to respond to any change, good or bad. Change in business is to be expected. Everything is business is subject to change. Market share, trends, employees, products and suppliers are all are subject to change. When change does come, be ready to act, have the vision to see things are they may be in the future. Recognize change and respond to it.

WORKING WITH THE GOVERNMENT

Try not to mix your income with politics. It is similar to teaching a pig to sing. Doing business with the government at almost any level is usually not good for your business. Most processes that are involved with selling to the government have no basis in real business. Profit and losses do not exist as they do in the real corporate business world. The processes currently in place were invented by people employed by the government to guarantee more work for them, and to insure their own employment for many years.

If you have a commercial product that the government can buy off your shelf, you may consider selling to them, but limit your risk. You most likely will not be paid on time and your product may be returned to you. Have your lawyer review any contract. Remember you will always risk being caught up in red tape to your disadvantage that can go on for decades.

Do What You Do Best

One of the biggest and costly mistakes I have seen business owners fall into and ultimately lead to the demise of the company, is diversification from the main product line of the business.

Company owners and CEO's need to know their main product, and why they are successful in selling this product. That is the secret of their success! Most small business fail within the first 2 years of existence. If your company has survived, and made money, you need to know why. You need to identify the things you are doing right and not only the things you do wrong. If you are unable to identify exactly what you have done right. (This is a common occurrence with many businesses, sometimes luck is involved in success) you will need to find out what you have been doing that has made you successful. Survey and customer satisfaction cards can be sent out with products or distributed to clients. Finding your strengths and weaknesses will always allow you to see your business in more depth.

Straying too far from your main product or service can be dangerous to the welfare of your business. Many companies have been dragged under by the costly mistakes of adding additional lines or products that have eaten the profits of your main product. While it is admirable and healthy for a business to grow, growing too fast can be catastrophic. Introducing new products, adding new product lines, can be very costly if you have not researched your market. If the product fails it will cost you money.

Sometimes it is cheaper to buy a business that specializes in the product that you wish to add to your product line. It can be added as a division of your business if it proves to be successful. It is important to retain the sales and marketing talent with this business. It is almost like buying out the competition. It can save years of market research and product development. The business you buy will already have a record with the product and proven sales.

Another option to add a product line with limited risk is to hire a retired executive that has brought a similar product to market. You need to find someone with enough experience that they can be depended on to see the current market and be able to adapt to your product. It is critical that you know the capabilities of the person you hire to head this product development. They must have a proven history with similar products.

Final Steps

In saving corporate money there are basic steps to follow. Know where your money is and what you are spending it on. Find ways to cut these costs to increase the health of the business. Plan on growth, but also plan on lean times. Stay informed and be prepared. The objective of any business is to minimize your risk of losing money while growing your product and market. The key to running a very successful corporation is to keep your costs low, while constantly striving and searching for new ways to increase operating efficiencies and income. Spend less than you are making.

A true leader is always able to look, listen, think, and solve problems outside the box. To make ethical decisions that are not self-serving, and allow the ongoing existence and profitable growth of a business.

References

Tzu, Sun _The Art of War_ Published by The Military Service Publishing Company, Harrisburg, Pennsylvania, 1944.

Machiavelli, Nicolo _The Prince_. N.p.: Written c. 1505, published 1515, translated by W. K. Marriott.

Taylor, Frederick W. _The Principals of Scientific Management_. Published 1911 in Norton Library

About The Author

Consultant and entrepreneur, R. E. Manchester has owned several businesses in Connecticut, worked with government agencies and with High Tech Corporations. Over the past twenty years she pioneered early computer cable manufacturing, followed by retail firms.

In the corporate environment she has worked with IPOs and Fortune 500 Companies. Her clients have included World Bank, Yale University and NASA. She has participated in local politics and remains a consultant.

She is currently involved with small business development, real estate investment, along with expanding a market of management information for business, finance and real estate. Ms. Manchester has been a guest speaker on business ethics at Sacred Heart University, Fairfield, CT.

How to Contact Us

Contact us via our website at:

www.SavingtheCorpDollar.com

or

Saving the Corporate Dollar
Post Office Box 1102
Fairfield, CT 06825